COUNTER_READINGS OF THE BODY   Edited by Daniel Neugebauer, with contributions by Olympia Bukkakis, María do Mar Castro Varela, Rain Demetri, Sabine Mohamed, Bonaventure Soh Bejeng Ndikung, Olave Nduwanje, Jules Sturm, and Julius Thissen

Counter_Readings of the Body

**Edited by
Daniel Neugebauer**

Contents

Counter_Readings of the Body

In search of possibilities for reading the world in novel ways, it is no coincidence that the body comes into view. Body semiotics and body epistemologies—or simply: body alphabets—construct identities, actions, power relations, communities.

This volume revolves around the construction and deconstruction of bodies through glances. The experience of everyday life provides the setting. Here, the human body appears as a sign system, an archive, a fiction, a projection screen, or an alphabet. The gaze, by contrast, appears as an adversary, a knife, the "evil eye," an instrument of power, the *male gaze*—incompetent or fleeting, it may itself be lost from sight. Who is subject, who object? Who creates or (de)constructs which realities? To extricate the body from this field of normative, evaluating, subjugating gazes is the aim of the texts and images assembled in this volume; they serve as mirrors that deflect views, perspectives, and ideas, making otherwise implicit and explicit reading procedures intelligible.

This, however, is less about flesh-and-blood bodies than about ways of reading, perceptions, and learning processes related to the physical manifestation of humans. Why is body language often mentioned, while reading bodies is never explicitly addressed or even formalized as corpoliteracy? It is my hope that social emancipation, gender diversity, postcolonial pedagogy or alternative cultural histories and techniques can be productively discussed in this context. The contributions in this volume are intended to provide suggestions—for unlearning, new learning, relearning.

The neologism "corpoliteracy" is derived from the team of Bonaventure Soh Bejeng Ndikung, founder and artistic director of Berlin art space SAVVY Contemporary. In *aneducation*—published on the occasion of documenta 14—he describes his interest in the "the possibility of a corpoliteracy—an effort to contextualize the body as a platform, stage, site, and medium of learning, a structure or organ that acquires, stores, and disseminates knowledge. This concept implies that the body, in sync with, but also independent of, the brain, has the potential to memorize and pass on/down acquired knowledge through performativity, through the prism of movement, dance and rhythm."

Another strategy of activating knowledge is eloquent resistance. Olave Nduwanje's activist poetry pleads, screams, howls, and lashes out to ward off biting glances from her body, which is read as "different." For her it is a matter of life and death. In a cultural studies analysis, Jules Sturm notes a failure in the social ability to see, which in its sleep produces monsters (but through this failure also clears the space for a new, tactile, and oneiric way of seeing): illustrator Rain Demetri translates the monsters into a self-defined visuality spanning a speculative arc between the textual contributions. Which social learning processes are necessary to defeat the monsters? Olympia Bukkakis has a solution: With her call for the abolition of all Men, she delivers a proposal for a radical recoding of society that is as sharp-witted as it is sharp-tongued. Yet the photographic works of Julius Thissen resurrect the doomed masculinities—radically transformed. María do Mar Castro Varela and Sabine Mohamed of bildungsLab* put collective focus on Afrofuturism as a school of seeing, making constructive suggestions for new "vision-building concepts"—in the sense of a politics of repair.

Visual habits and binary norms are attacked, softened, and supplemented from all sides to show that cultural processes (understood as interactions in analogue or digital cultural zones) always involve a scanning of bodies, avatars, identities for signs of gender, class, digital or surgical processing, sexual orientation, ethnicity, dis_ability, age, etc., in order to categorize, de-, or revalue them. This means that cultural actors and cultural institutions must take responsibility for strategically thwarting these processes and working on alternatives. Being corpoliterate, then, means being able to perform a complex, intersectional reading of bodies and to develop corpoliteracy as a practice of respect.

Daniel Neugebauer

Translated from the German by Kevin Kennedy

DO NOT READ THIS BODY

DO NOT READ THIS BODY!
DO NOT READ MY BODY!
DO NOT READ ME!

I mean it: Do not read this body!

I can feel your scanning eyes, your knowing eyes, your pretentious eyes, your judgmental eyes. I can feel them on my skin, on the curve of my lips, on the edges of my frown, on the heights of my cheekbones.

I can feel your eyes. They reach for the shape of my knuckles, the contour of my cock in my squirt. I can feel them. Your eyes. They are hungry.

They press on my soft belly, wondering what I eat,
They press on my hard skull, calculating what I am thinking,
They press on my beating heart, guessing what I am feeling.

I raise my palms outwards, in self-defense.

I clench my fists, threateningly, pleadingly: "Do No Read this Body!"

Do you hear the fear in my voice? Do you feel the despair?
Do you understand it?

Have you learned to fear a knowing look? Does a confident gaze terrify you too? Do you also fear the violence of eyes that read?

Eyes that will dissect, assemble, categorize and archive? Scientific eyes; machine eyes with embedded algorithms; artificially intelligent eyes.

Do you know them? Do you fear them? The eyes that monitor, police, judge, record, and assign blame.

I can feel them everywhere, your searching eyes, your reading eyes, your substitute eyes, your eyes.

A lover once told me: "I see you."

My heart froze, my mind ran, my body wanted to fight! We wrestled!

I held them down and said: "This sounds like a threat; it is a claim on me. I rather you would just look. Just look! This 'seeing' puts me at a disadvantage. I can't see myself! Mirrors and selfies offer poor reflections of me; reversed facsimiles, two-dimensional portraits. You are a poor mirror too. In your eyes, I am a greater sum than my parts, or an unknowable quantum element."

They fought back, anchored me down, lying on my belly, my arsehole exposed, I pleaded: "I rather you would just look. Just look! Bear witness, don't claim me! Pick a place beside me, and let me do the seeing. I look from the inside out. It is cozy and dark in here. Inside here, it is also lonely and scary. From inside, this body moves me from space to space, gaze to gaze. And things happen: happy things, sad things, violent things, funny things. You happened, you happy, sad, violent, funny thing. Your body happened to mine."

I bucked and kicked, reversed and spun, they lost their grip. And when I was freed, I sang: "When you kiss me, I close my eyes to move you deeper inside, to touch you inside; to be inside with you. Just look, and when you can't bear to look anymore, kiss me, be with me inside."

I am an animated speaker. I speak with my hands and wrists. My mouth savors the words, my head moves with the confidence of a steady train of thought. I frown on cue; I laugh with nuance; my smile punctuates inflections. My back arches as I bend my body into strategic exclamation marks.

At this very moment, I am seated at the edge of my seat, as if to reach you, through the walls. I want to be near to you, in thought and in body. Speaking stretches every part of my body, every tendon, every muscle is activated, as I postulate, explain, defend, persuade, and conclude.

Now that you can't see me, I wonder whether the agitation of my body will scare you less. My Black body, undulating, tensing, demanding attention, disciplining you, teaching you, accusing you, wanting more and better from you. Angry Black bodies are your proverbial monsters in the closet, the boogeymen and boogey-women hiding under your bed, hungry to right the wrongs of history with the sharp blade of revenge. Now that you can't see me, will you hear me better?

Our bodies form a static of intuitive information, projections, assumptions. I know you can't hear me, because I can't hear you through it. Your white body–I fear it, your cisgendered body–I reject it, your male body–I fuck it, your straight body–I hate it, your thin body–I reject it. Your white body–I hide from it, your cisgendered body–I envy it, your male body–I let it in me, your straight body–I rely on it. Your white body–I hate it. Your cisgendered body–I lick it. Your male body–I spank it. Your thin body–I fight it.

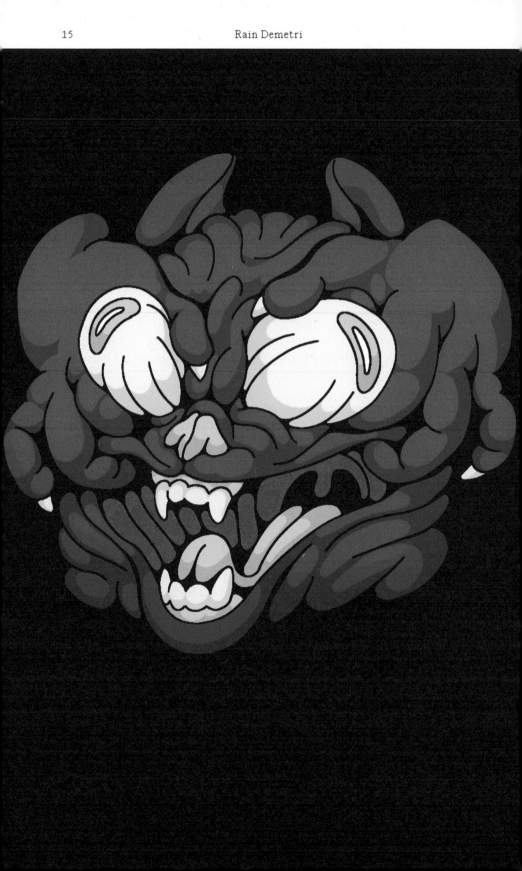

Tell me: do you feel seen? Would you like me to see you? Do you want me to read you? To know you?

Tell me: What gives you away? Is it what you are wearing? Or how you stand? Or who you stand with? Is it who you fuck? Is it how you love? Is it the blue of your hair? The pink of your glitter? Or is it the black of your boots? What does the sweat and cum drying up on your Berghain outfits say about you?

Tell me: What do you know about yourself? Are you an open book? Does your cover deceive people? Are you deeper than you look like? Are you kinder than you seem? Are you stronger than you appear?

Tell me: Are all your pages written out? If I read you, would you thank me for it? Would you love me then? Would you love yourself then?

Tell me: If I read you? If I read you and found your prose ugly? If I read you and found your plot predictable and boring? If I read you and found your metaphors wrong and your tone aggressive? If I read you and found the rhythm of your story flat?

Tell me: Would you change your story then? Would you rewrite yourself? Would you reconsider the logic of your past, reassess the depth of your traumas, restructure the texture of your loves, repaint the colors of your faults?

Tell me: Would you plagiarize to be interesting? Would you plagiarize to be beautiful? Would you plagiarize to be deep? Would you plagiarize to be relevant? Would you steal storylines, plot twists, and characters to belong, to be valued, to be seen?

Tell me: How do you know you are not plagiarizing right now? How do you know you haven't edited your story countless times? What is true about you? What do you know about you?

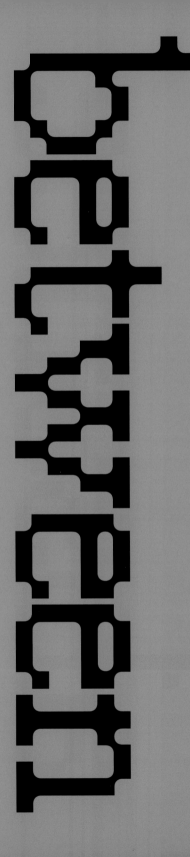

between

A white savior once told me: "I don't see color. You could be white, yellow, purple, for all I care."

I said, with blame and accusation in my voice: "That's bullshit! Of course you see my skin color! You see it. What you refuse to do, however, is to acknowledge that my Blackness is targeted, hunted, disregarded, hated, feared, desired, excluded, dismissed, neglected. What you refuse to acknowledge is that there are endless ways in which my Blackness is violenced and violated. What you refuse to acknowledge is that it benefits you. What you refuse to acknowledge is that you can, should, and must be held accountable for the benefits you accrue and for your inaction."

I said, with authority and anger in my eyes: "You do see that I am Black. You see it, I know it and you know it. The effort you do to not acknowledge my Blackness is violent. It is self-serving, it is inexcusable. It is no cause for congratulations, for applause. I will give you no pats on the back, no approval. It is lazy, violent, and untruthful."

I said, with reproach and scorn on my lips: "I know what you really want to say. You want to say: 'I am not concerned or involved in this racism business. By the sheer power of my will and the grace of my intention, I have opted out of racism. See, here, this force field I have magicked around me. It nullifies the reality and consequences of racism within ten meters of my white body."

I said, with resolve and force, as I snapped: "You think that I need to be elevated from my Blackness. You put on your blindfold to recognize me as valid, worthy, and valuable. You think that rejecting the color of my skin elevates me to the alabaster halls of humanity. You know what that is: It is racism! It is the belief that the melanin of my skin devalues me. A belief that has you rushing to ignore it, to un-see it, to erase it."

I said, with false certainty: "I reject your elective color-blindness, for I will not tolerate to be diminished. My skin is mine, it is mine. You cannot, you will not, flay my skin off. I will not allow it: I am complete."

I have been reading Roxane Gay's *Hunger* this week. It is my second attempt. The first time, I could not get past the chapter in which she describes the gang rape. I could not get past that.

This time, I am resolved to read her memoir of her body. But her prose remains hard and difficult to move through. It is barbed, you see. It is sharp. It stings and cuts. Every page leaves me bloody and exhausted.

I feel thrown. Thrown back into my fat body. I carry and nurture a fat body too. You might not know this, but fat bodies need a lot of care and nurture. My fat body is a different kind of fat body than Roxane Gay's. But what I think we have in common, is what our fat bodies do for us.

I am impressed by the fact that she deliberately and intentionally made her body fat. She says so. She says that she wanted to make her body into a body that was so fat, so big, that it could not be broken again; that it could not be violated again. I am impressed that she knew, that she strategized and executed.

These last few years, I have been catching up with knowing, with understanding, with acknowledging the strategies my body chose to protect me. The choices I made to be safe. Safe from everyone and most things. But especially, safe from your desire for my body. Your hunger for my body. Your need to touch it, press on it, squeeze it, pull at it, lick it, salivate on it, bite into it, to enter it. To enter me. Without so much as an invitation, or permission.

Your desire and lust has always thrown me. It has thrown me out of my body. And I am runner, you see. When your hunger throws me, I keep running. I don't run into the recesses of my mind. I run out, towards the sky, towards the lights, I run out of my body.

All that throwing and running has weakened the ties, links, and chains to my body. A lifelong of being thrown and running outwards, will do that. It will loosen your hold to your body... Or is it your body's hold on you...? It will turn you into a frequent visitor to your body. I have become a guest, a reluctant stranger, huddled in my body.

I stopped knowing that my body anticipated to be broken, over and over again. That my body geared itself up for violence. That my body grew to withstand the attacks that would not stop coming. I am proud of my body for having taken the lead of protecting us. I am sorry I ran out, too often. I didn't help you grow, I was absent.

But here we are now: I have grown. I am fat. I am big. I am strong. They will try to break us, dear body, but you made us so very hard to break. You made us ready to fight back. And that is beautiful, so very beautiful.

Bonaventure Soh Bejeng Ndikung

CORPOLITERACY[1]

O my body, make of me always a man who questions!
—Frantz Fanon, *Black Skin, White Masks*

But they jeered one and all and said:
This is only the night of bonfires
We need dancers around the blaze
Acrobats and drummers, stilt dancers
And, listen carefully, lest you forget
—Olu Oguibe, *The Youth Who Dances*

An Igbo proverb states that when we dance we express who we were, who we are, and who we want to be. Time is compressed and telescoped teleologically to contain and express the past, the present and the future in one fluid kinaesthetic moment.
—Esiaba Irobi, *The Philosophy of the Sea*

In a December 2017 presentation for the symposium "That Around Which the Universe Revolves—On the Rhythmanalysis of Memory, Times, Bodies in Space,"[2] filmmaker and theorist Trinh T. Minh-Hà proposed rhythm as the door between body and mind. She later expatiated on this proposal, referring to the concept of the embodied mind common to many Afro-Asiatic philosophies. I have been thinking of rhythm within this analogy: Everything that leads to or induces a rhythm, facilitates a passage through, an inscription in, a writing on, a recording, and a spelling on and of that embodied mind.[3] If the body

1   This essay is reprinted with the kind permission of the author, editors, and publisher of the original publication: Sepake Angiama, Clare Butcher, Alkisti Efthymiou, Anton Kats, Arnisa Zequo (eds.), *Eine Erfahrung - documenta* 14. Berlin: Archive Books, 2019, pp. 89–96; English version: *aneducation - documenta* 14, pp. 114–21.

2   Trinh T. Minh-Hà, "On Fourth Dimension," presentation for SAVVY Contemporary's discursive and performative symposium, "That Around Which the Universe Revolves—On the Rhythmanalysis of Memory, Times, Bodies in Space," Hebbel am Ufer, Berlin, December 3, 2017.

3   Henri Lefebvre says: "Everywhere where there is interaction between a place, a time and an expenditure of energy, there is rhythm." See his *Rhythmanalysis: Space, Time, and Everyday Life*, trans. Stuart Elden and Gerald Moore. London: Continuum, 2004, p. 15. The body, according

is the mind, then it has the capacity to learn and memorize. Every movement in space and time—be it a walk, a dance, or otherwise, every gesticulation, every exercise of the muscles and the cells that make up the body—is possibly remembered. But every intervention on the body—scarifications, tattoos, scars, or injuries—trigger that process of memory.

I explore the possibility of a *corpoliteracy*—an effort to contextualize the body as a platform, stage, site, and medium of learning, a structure or organ that acquires, stores, and disseminates knowledge. This concept implies that the body, in sync with, but also independent of, the brain, has the potential to memorize and pass on/down acquired knowledge through performativity—the prism of movement, dance, and rhythm.

It is common practice that when the Nguemba peoples—like many other peoples on the African continent and beyond—dance, they invoke and embody certain totems important to particular families or societies at large. The elephant, lion, monkey, or snake dances not only mimic typical movements of these animals but also summon the spirits that connect the human to his/her animal. These dances, which are usually performed in groups, then serve a purpose beyond that of mere entertainment and pleasure: The dances become sites that enliven rituals, spaces of spiritual communication and bonding; the bodies that perform are the tools through or with which the rituals are practiced. To the accompaniment of ritual music, the movements of the legs, arms, and the rest of the body invoke certain spirits, and through repetition and reiteration, a certain degree of automation is achieved. Dance becomes a means through which rituals are expressed—or better still—dance is the ritual. Through dance one can communicate with certain spirits and convoke them for the purposes of worship and appeasement. It is no surprise that in the performativity of dance, more often than not, the dancer is catapulted into a temporary state of ecstasy. The etymological roots of ecstasy are not unimportant: "elation" comes from Old French, *estaise* (ecstasy, rapture), derived from the Late Latin *extasis* and the Greek *ekstasis* (entrancement, astonishment, insanity; any displacement or removal

to Lefebvre, is a collection of rhythms with different tunes that result from history, facilitated by calling on all senses, drawing on breathing, and blood circulation, just as much as heartbeats and speech utterances, as landmarks of this experience.

from the proper place). It is this rapture, displacement, and removal from a particular space—in dance, the displacement from one's own body, the possibility of an out-of-body state—that becomes very interesting: trance as state; transcendence via the exalted state of body and soul when dancing.

Besides the spiritual and ritual aspects of dance, performing has obviously been a way for people to write or encode their own histories. Wars or other challenges faced by a group of people take form as dance moves, or are integrated into costumes and music. Battle techniques, loss of life, or moments of victory are re-performed, passed from one generation to another, as with the Mbaya dance or Capoeira. Group dances often reveal moments of encounter. Encountering of a new religion, for example, can lead to the appropriation of those religious signs, as happened with the appearance of the Catholic cross in the Pépé Kallé and Nyboma dances. Encountering new technologies also gives rise to dance moves: arms open wide can symbolize a plane; or the move in the Pédalé dance in which dancers mimic cycling. There is more work to be done exploring the body's performative role in dance with respect to the conservation, portrayal, and dissemination of peoples' histories and that of places and events—dance as a method of historicity, an alternative writing of history, as historiography. The challenge is to acknowledge dance performance as a medium—in its own right—that can reflect with veracity, authenticity, and actuality historical knowledge claims.

Through dances like the Juba, the Chica, or Calenda, one learns about particular times in history: repressions, racial relations, resistances, resilience, and more. The body of the dancer is the witness. The witness' narrative—especially when the witness is silent—occurs through performativity. Every performance is to a certain degree a re-experience and re-witnessing, rather than just observation. Through dance the observer becomes witness. In "Consciousness is Total, Pure Energy" from the Tibetan Buddhist *The Book of Wisdom*, we learn:

> [T]he observer means the subjective, and the observed means the objective. The observer means that which is outside the observed, and the observer also means that which is inside.
> The inside and the outside can't be separate; they are together, they can only be together. When this togetherness, or rather

oneness, is experienced, the witness arises. You cannot practice the witness. If you practice the witness you will be practicing only the observer, and the observer is not the witness.[4]

It is this oneness of the observer and observed, inside and outside, that makes dance as a method and practice particularly interesting at this juncture. In Osho practice, it is said that while the scientist is an observer, the mystic is a witness. The dancer, too, could be considered a witness in this light: their ability to perform the processuality of making histories, and offer testimony, collapses the separation of inside from outside.

Through dance and the accompanying music, sociopolitical realities are embodied, portrayed, and sometimes even processed psychologically and somatically. During the avian influenza outbreak in West Africa in 2008, DJ Lewis released a popular track in the Ivory Coast called "Grippe Aviaire"; the dance moves in the music video spread like wild fire among the young and old alike. In nightclubs, offices, public spaces, people dangled their half-raised arms, eyes wide open, evoking movements of chickens with bird flu. That same year another Ivory Coast artist, DJ Zidane, at the height of maltreatment of prisoners in Guantanamo on the other side of the Atlantic, invented the Guantanamo dance. Teenagers gathered in public spaces dancing as though handcuffed or crippled. Art engulfed sociopolitical reality; histories and knowledges were embodied in dance, as were societal sentiments, traumas, joys, and fears. Dance is not about the individual, but the community—the commons. As Léopold Sédar Senghor put it:

'Je pense donc je suis'; écrivait Descartes. [...] Le Negro-africain pourrait dire: 'Je sens l'Autre, je danse l'Autre, donc je suis.'
Or danser, c'est créer, surtout si la danse est d'amour. C'est, en tout cas, le meilleur mode de connaissance.
'I think, therefore, I am,' Descartes writes. [...] The Negro-African could say, 'I feel, I dance the other, therefore I am.'
To dance is to create, especially if the dance is of love. In any event, it is the best way to know.[5]

4   See Osho, *The Book of Wisdom: The Heart of Tibetan Buddhism*. New York: Osho Media International, 2009 [1979].
5   Léopold Sédar Senghor, *Liberté* 1: *Négritude et humanisme*. Paris: Éditions du Seuil, 1964, p. 259. Translation by Bonaventure Soh Bejeng Ndikung.

Senghor—the poet, philosopher, and politician—points out a few important things here. Dance is about creation and it is about knowledge. But maybe most importantly, dance seems to be about connecting with the other, about communion, a group action. Dance, in all the aforementioned functions, manifests itself most effectively when one "dances the other." Dance is a social phenomenon. From Agwara dance, Bikutsi, Coupé Décalé, and Zouglou, or circle, contra, or square dances, to street dances like breakdancing in which the crew becomes a surrogate family, dance reflects sociopolitical realities, current and historical affairs, and needs a community to be lived and experienced. One can find solace in the dance crew, and share happiness among birds of a feather. The crew is a place for mentorship, often crucial to community building. Hip-hop, dancehall moves, krump, and many other urban forms of dance offer a degree of social credibility to the dancers—not only because they dance well, but because of their affiliation with the crew.

In *Dance and Politics: Moving Beyond Boundaries*, Dana Mills writes about dance as a means of communication and as writing. Her argument can be radically summarized as follows: There are more languages than just verbal; human beings have found manifold ways to communicate with each other; and dance is an embodied language, a form of communication between bodies in motion. As such, the language of dance adheres to different rules and structures than those of verbal language. Dance is the way those subjects perform their equality before expressing themselves verbally. There are clashes between verbal and non-verbal languages. At the meeting point between dance and verbal languages, different symbolic and political frameworks collide, underscoring the presence of two forms of language. Political dance, or the constitution of dance as a world that does not require language, creates a shared embodied space between dancer and spectator, between equality and plurality; equality of bodies allows them to speak with each other unmediated by words; plurality of human beings pushes them to express themselves through their bodies. Through these two aspects, dance is inscribed upon the body. The body is altered by inscription, informing it of communities and possibilities—a dancing body is never alone but conversing with an Other. But dancing subjects can transcend the boundaries of their communities and live in more than one world—both that constituted by dance as a method of communication and by words as a method of expression. As a practice that goes beyond boundaries, dance challenges demarcations between communities erected by verbal language, transcending spaces created by words: this happens at the moment dancers gain entry into a community larger than the one to which they were assigned, attesting to the equality of bodies.[6]

Dance is a sociopolitical method and practice, a means of writing, narrating, and disseminating histories. It is a corporeal phenomenon that can be a catalyst for building communities and challenge and transcend the boundaries of societies and languages. The dancing body becomes the witness, a *somatotestimonium*—the body in a dance performance and the movements employed as a formal statement are equivalent to a written, spoken, eyewitness, or earwitness account, proof of a spatiotemporal reality.

The above led me to develop the concepts of *corpoliteracy* and *corpoepistemology*, involving the study of the nature and extent of bodily knowledge in dance performance, as well as how the body and dance performance produce, enact, inscribe, and propagate knowledges. Like epistemological studies in general, it is important to analyze bodies employed in dance in relation to notions of truth or belief. Corpoepistemology focuses on manifestations of politicized, sexualized, genderized, and racialized bodies in performativity. Corpoepistemology is preoccupied with questions like: What is bodily knowledge? How is bodily knowledge acquired? How is bodily knowledge expressed in dance performances? How can the observer of a performance decipher and relate to these bodily knowledges? If rhythm and dance provide the structure for a form of such bodily knowledge, what are the limits?

6   See Dana Mills, *Dance and Politics: Moving Beyond Boundaries*. Manchester: Manchester University Press, 2017.

Literacy Embodied

The Word for Body left my Body.
—Johanna Hedva, 2019

I can feel your eyes. Do not read this body!
—Olave Nduwanje, 2019

Among other things, my writing is about "looking" as an embodied, subjective, and cultural practice of reading bodies. In my theorizing, I propose to consider "looking" at bodies not as a mere physiological process, but as a complexly constructed, schooled, cultured, and discriminatory, yet also sensual and potentially subversive grammar of making sense of our own and others' bodies. I thereby bring into dialogue two realms importantly involved in understanding bodies: visuality (What do I see?) and epistemology (What do I know?). No matter how productive the relation between these two realms in itself is, I am exploring the misgivings or the incoherencies in them, as I believe that it is in the *failure* of making sense of bodies where we find the potential to read bodies differently. Furthermore, I contest the Western intellectual mindset of so-called *objective* seeing and knowing, which posits the body always as object (of vision and knowledge). I therefore started to train myself in how to inquire about what I might fail to see or know of bodies and rather to ask *How* do I see? and *How* do I know? Thereby I was taking into account that processes of knowing and seeing are both in themselves bodily practices, which are necessarily dependent on the very "apparatus" of seeing and knowing: the body itself.

> My aim is not to develop an all-inclusive theory of the body, but to try to let the body in art be a mirror for theoretical accounts—accounts that ideally attempt to draw on their own blind spots to develop new forms of seeing and knowing.[1]

I understand visuality as a theoretical as well as an embodied field for reflection about our various practices of seeing and reading

1   Jules Sturm, *Bodies We Fail: Productive Embodiments of Imperfection*, vol. 38. Bielefeld: transcript Verlag, 2014, p. 21.

bodies. In my writing, I attempt to expose and learn from some of the failures of our common ways of seeing and reading the bodies of others and suggest conceptualizations of how to "look otherwise." I consider various odd, queer, and uneasy ways of looking as alternative body-reading practices. Some resonate urgently with Olave Nduwanje's plea: "Do not read this body. [...] I rather you would just look. Just look! This seeing business puts me at too great a disadvantage."[2] The systemic disadvantage of being "seen" as a Black, trans, disabled, sick, migrant, fat, small, queer, or Other body, might only be countered by discarding our claim to literacy—the claim to knowledge—from our "seeing" habits. We might instead need to recognize what we *fail* to see in/on/of/for these bodies and "just look."

[I] explore the effects of what I term 'productive failure.' Failure is a form of deficiency when an anticipated action is not achieved, or is accomplished in a different way than anticipated. Failure also signifies an inability to meet and conform tocertain norms. These two most common definitions of failure are negatively connoted and depend on forms of achievement that assume and promote functionality, structural sameness, efficiency, positivity, evolution, and progress. As such, I find the effects of failure not particularly productive for critical thought, since they can only be measured in dichotomous terms such as good and bad, or better and worse.[3]

2   Olave Nduwanje, "DO NOT READ THIS BODY," in this volume, pp. 9–19 (originally presented at the Haus der Kulturen der Welt, Berlin, September 14, 2019) https://soundcloud.com/search?q=Olave%20 Nduwanje, accessed 29 October 2020.
3   Sturm, *Bodies We Fail*, pp. 21–23.

I am therefore proposing to embrace those aspects of "seeing" which are commonly repressed for the sake of clarity, proficiency, and power, yet necessary for critical body-reading capacities: partial blindness, vulnerable looking, nonappearance, and failed visual literacy. I take Nduwanje's appeal for "just looking" as an important reminder (for my own theoretical analysis also) to stay acutely aware of the potential violence our "seeing" inflicts when serving literacy by "dissecting, assembling, categorizing."[4] The aim of developing less violent *corpo*-literate practices must therefore inevitably also counter the mastery of literacy, which is to grasp, compare, divide, dichotomize, classify—to know. Corpoliterate practices of seeing must consequently comprise the simultaneous *failures* of visual and literate practices: obscurity, opacity, blindness, blurredness, wildness, nonsense, and uncertainty.

> Art that motivates embodied reflection, or involved looking,
> not only inaugurates an ethically valuable form of looking—
> by appealing to the viewer's responsibility in the creation of the
> image—but it also makes room for the visual object's agency
> in the perceived image. [...] This risk of looking at the other also
> involves *being seen by* the other, which adds to the act of look-
> ing; the awareness that one always looks from a contingent onto-
> logical position. Consequently, the awareness of one's posi-
> tional and thus perspectival viewpoint toward the other threat-
> ens the ostensibly objective and unidirectional way of knowing
> what one sees.[5]

Yet, how can we not only *postulate* such a travesty of visuality and literacy for a more generous reading of bodies but also likewise *embody* it? How can we learn a new practice characterized essentially by the refusal to engage in the usual formations of learning, like acquiring proficiency? How can writing about these practices help to translate them into our everyday lives? Nora Sternfeld has importantly recognized the impact of "unlearning" for the transmission of alternative knowledges, to which I account embodied knowledges. Sternfeld writes that unlearning must be understood as a tentative

4   Nduwanje, "DO NOT READ THIS BODY"
5   Sturm, *Bodies We Fail*, p. 81.

rehearsal of disrupting learnt practices and habits—a rehearsal without promise and prone to failure, yet fundamental for development of new corporeal routines: "In this sense, unlearning is also an exercise where we slowly, gradually break with learned practices and habits of making difference based on dominant power relations that are already inscribed in our habits, bodies and actions. This is indeed an incredibly difficult task, which is also riddled with uncertainties."[6]

In another context, Jack Halberstam calls for the exercise of low theory, which here comprises a critique of institutionalized intellectual activity as well as celebration of the unknown, the "silly," the failed. In the spirit of what Halberstam calls "the queer art of failure,"[7] I developed the paradigm of the "good enough,"[8] which helps to dismantle the binary opposition between corporeal ideals and bodily imperfection. The notion of the "good enough" reveals how the ideal can only ever be an approximation and never actually be achievable. For visuality, the conception of the "good enough" means to reject corporeal ideals while embracing physical approximation, partiality, obscurity, opacity, indeterminacy, improvisation, and "unreality."[9] In the logic of the "good enough," the failure to fulfill the ideal body/image is to achieve the "possibility of productive vision—of an eye capable of seeing something other than what is given to be seen, and over which the self does not hold absolute sway."[10]

> Failure is here expressed as producing something new and other, through a partial loss of control for the autonomous subject. Productive vision is thus built not only on failing ideality, but also on failing the self-sufficient and homogeneous subject.[11]

6   Nora Sternfeld, "Learning Unlearning," *CuMMA Papers*, no. 20 (2016), trans. Erika Doucette, p. 10, https://cummastudies.files.wordpress.com /2016/09/cumma-papers-20.pdf, accessed October 26, 2020.
7   Judith Halberstam, *The Queer Art of Failure*. Durham, NC: Duke University Press, 2011.
8   Kaja Silverman, *The Threshold of the Visible World*. London: Routledge, 1996, p. 4.
9   Ibid., p. 55.
10   Ibid., p. 227.
11   Sturm, *Bodies We Fail*, p. 22.

In my engagement with failure, I understand "the body not as magical nut to crack or foreign planet to explore, but as intimate companion to love and cherish."[12] I believe that "the body invites this loving relationship because of, and not despite, its emblematic negativity, its vulnerability, its deficient stability, and, last but not least, its mortality."[13] Thus, by incorporating the possibility of failure into projects related to physicality and humanity, my writing aimed to not only expose the body's limitations, but also to extend the body's dimensions. What fails us, therefore, are not bodies, but our ways of understanding them: Our current cultural practices, of seeing, reading, and reinscribing bodies with meaning, fail the possibilities of knowing corporeality otherwise. To engage with these possibilities must involve new ways of learning. Cameroonian curator Bonaventure Ndikung uses the concept of corpoliteracy to ascribe to the body a special function in re-learning: "corpoliteracy [is] an effort to contextualize the body as a platform, stage, site, and medium of learning, a structure or organ that acquires, stores, and disseminates knowledge. This concept implies that the body, in sync with, but also independent of, the brain, has the potential to memorize and pass on/down acquired knowledge through performativity—the prism of movement, dance, and rhythm."[14]

> When reading *Frankenstein*,[15] Judith Halberstam asks:
> 'Do I read or am I written? Am I monster or monster maker?
> Am I monster hunter or the hunted? Am I human or other?'[16]

---

12   Ibid., p. 17.

13   Ibid.

14   Bonaventure Soh Bejeng Ndikung, "CORPOLITERACY," in this volume, pp. 21–26.

15   Mary Shelley, *Frankenstein, Or The Modern Prometheus.* Oxford: Oxford University Press, 1998 [1831].

16   Sturm, *Bodies We Fail*, p. 35. The quote is taken from Judith Halberstam, *Skin Shows: Gothic Horror and the Technology of Monsters.* Durham, NC: Duke University Press, 1995, p. 36.

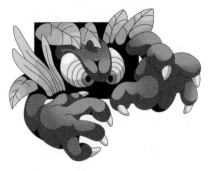

As my body gave me access to ways of failing that are productive, I asked myself whether my own body is the most radical and proximate access I have to the failings of my cultural practices. I also ask myself: How can I use this body for productively failing my learning, my writing, my speaking, my thinking, my reading, and my seeing?[17]

> Reading the monster is always linked to an act of imagination, an act of visualization.[18]

While unlearning my body's composure in space was a satisfying experience, I experience the practices involved in unlearning *ideas* as painful and depressing. That is, close reading is excruciatingly slow and seemingly ineffective when under the pressure of deadlines, output quotients, and financial or social rewards. Just as embodied writing disturbingly pushes against tediously acquired academic rules and routines; just as the empathic-affective analysis of vulnerable others exposes my own self to vulnerability; and just as the academic query of bodily failings in visual representation shatters my sense of clear sight.[19]

> The danger of visibility lies in its merely repeating the once-formed image of the conceptual cultural other to accommodate current hegemonic ideology and to eliminate deviation.[20]

17   See Jules Sturm, "Ways of Failing," *Digressions*, vol. 3, no. 2 (2019), special issue: The 'Failing' Body, pp. 1–4.
18   Sturm, *Bodies We Fail*, p. 39.
19   See Sturm, "Ways of Failing."
20   Sturm, *Bodies We Fail*, p. 128.

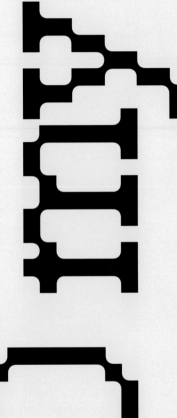

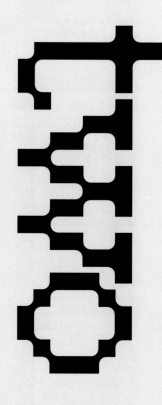

Nevertheless, how can my *writing* be useful to imagine alternative grammars for revisualizing, dis-reading, and describing bodies in our current cultural landscape? By putting my writing into the hands and hearts of artists, educators, students, and other critical thinkers and doers, I attempt to lend my thoughts many voices, limbs, organs, desires, intensities, reverberations, passions, and a wild assemblage of (mis)perceptions. The recognition that others are better at translating my writing into realms of knowing has otherwise helped me to believe in my writing as a transitory medium to achieve a more embodied view of the world. Artist Angelo Custódio has given voice to my thoughts such as when he writes: "There are thoughts and their noisy embodiments. They move muscles and hair; they produce saliva, sweat, hormones. Thoughts are embodied and [...] never fully in control. We are just a multiplicity of visible embodiments of thoughts, of perceptions and autonomous reactions. And if there is no silence within this communication, there must be an exchange, a flow of negotiating knowledge."[21] It is in this sense, therefore, that here I am sharing scraps of writing from *Bodies We Fail*, as teasers or triggers for new grammars and visions of embodied lives of all dialects and vernaculars.

> [My analysis of visuality] suggests a parallel with speech: it assumes the act of looking to be communicative. To understand what one sees, one must recognize it as something that belongs to a visual system, which is shared and communicated among others. But what happens with the visual stimuli that we do not understand? Many of these, I suggest, unsettle the viewer, since they cannot easily be attributed to some other, foreign language: it is not commonly believed that there exists more than one visual sign system. Instead, un- or misrecognized images are banished to the world of the other, the deformed, the disabled, the unnatural, or the objectified.[22]

21   Angelo Custódio, "The Creature in the Crack continued," *Digressions*, vol. 3, no. 2, (2019), special issue: The 'Failing' Body, pp. 58–85, here p. 60.
22   Sturm, *Bodies We Fail*, pp. 63–4.

In my earlier writing, I had not yet come across the concept of corporeal literacy, which would have helped me in that I would have realized that any theory *of* the body must also attempt to become, at least partially, an "embodied theory." I would have recognized that the means, through which I compose my thoughts in writing, are literate practices that comprise embodied elements. Cultural theorist and dramaturg Maaike Bleeker has described the means of composing thought as "corporeal literacy" as a perspective which establishes an important connection between literate practices and corporeality: "[Corporeal Literacy] brings out the performative character of processes of perception and cognition, focusing particularly on the corporeal dimension of [literate] practices."[23] Bleeker continues: "[More] than describing the capacity to read and write, corporeal literacy denotes culturally-specific synaesthetic modes of information processing brought about by culturally specific practices of noting down, storing and transmitting information. These practices, therefore, beyond simply providing useful tools, profoundly influence how we think and understand."[24] The concept of corporeal literacy adds a hitherto ignored dimension to my theoretical writing: that the process of how I construct meaning through theory is crucial to what this meaning can or cannot embody, what it can or cannot convey, and finally how it can or cannot help me to view bodies in a different light.

Paradoxically, what my earlier writings failed to do was to take account of the (dis-)embodiment of meaning-making through (academic) writing. It is indeed telling, yet not surprising, that I

23   Maaike Bleeker, "Corporeal Literacy: New Modes of Embodied
      Interaction in Digital Culture," in Sarah Bay-Cheng, Chiel Kattenbelt,
      Andy Lavender et al. (eds), *Mapping Intermediality in Performance*.
      Amsterdam: Amsterdam University Press, 2010, pp. 38–43, here p. 38.
24   Ibid., p. 40.

engaged in what is possibly considered the most "literate" form of cultural practice in modern Western societies, without considering the discrepancy between the embodied act of writing/typing and literacy's inherent tendency to erase the body's impact on such practice as writing. Communication theorist Carolyn Marvin makes an important observation about how, in writing, the body is actively repressed and thus neglected in the making of meaning: "A mark of literate competence is skill in disguising or erasing the contribution of one's own body to the process of textual production and practice."[25] The recognition that "[literate] acts aim at dissociating mind from body" and that "to practice literacy is, at the very least, to disguise and repudiate the body,"[26] is to question what literacy might achieve for bodies that refute categorization. For "[i]f literacy is not exclusively a mental skill, any conceptual shift to the notion of literacy as an embodied practice has important consequences."[27] Relating this notion of literacy to visuality, we should take care not to promote what is commonly called "visual literacy," a so-called competence that uncritically remains within and promotes hegemonic knowledge regimes. Instead, we must insist on engaging in practices of "embodied reflection," or "literacy *embodied*," a set of skills that simultaneously (synesthetically) involves aural, haptic, libidinal, visual, and mental abilities as much as their potential breakdowns.

> [I here] analyze the potential of absence for the representation
> of bodies that have not been overlooked but, rather, have been
> 'looked over' within the realm of a particular, discriminatory,
> and/or neglectful visual practice; a practice that has been
> formed by an economy of visibility, an aesthetic economy with
> political consequences for the construction of the image of
> the other. The other is fixed in and through the image that par-
> ticipates in a cultural fantasy that is often racist and sexist.
> I make use of the concept of absence as a tool to analyze the link
> between bodies and their absences, which is to say their
> images. If viewers are confronted with the negative aspect of
> visual presence in art, they become aware of the constructed

25   Carolyn Marvin, "The Body of the Text: Literacy's Corporeal Constant,"
      Quarterly Journal of Speech, vol. 80, no. 2 (1994), pp. 129–49, here p. 129.
26   Ibid., p. 132.
27   Ibid.

relation between living bodies and their representations. In my
view, the idea of absence disrupts the seeming coherence of
this relation, and helps to develop alternative ways of imaging
or imagining those bodies that have been subjected to repre-
sentational stereotyping and pictorial neglect.[28]

How must, how can my writing transform language, style, tone, vision,
and outlook to better incorporate embodied practices of all kinds into
its own making and breaking?

> I would [like to conclude with the] thematic of failure: as losers
> in the struggle to achieve coherence, self-sufficiency, success,
> efficiency, smoothness, perfection, competence, and legibility,
> 'failing bodies' have the capacity to seek out and possibly
> build new forms of desirable lives. In this study, failure is con-
> ceptualized as an engagement with and a finding of comfort
> in shifting grounds, obscure vision, oblique angles, imperfec-
> tions, dancing tables (Sara Ahmed), and in the art of unbe-
> coming (J. Halberstam). My aim has been to 'de-script' bodies
> (*ent-schreiben*) rather than to describe them (*beschreiben*),
> to disentangle them from normatively descriptive images,
> and to complicate simplified visions of our bodies. Bodies we
> fail are bodies we might ultimately learn to love.[29]

28   Sturm, *Bodies We Fail*, p. 122.
29   Ibid., p. 187, slightly modified. The sources for the references are Sara
      Ahmed, *Queer Phenomenology: Orientations, Objects, Others*. Durham,
      NC: Duke University Press, 2006, p. 164; and Judith Halberstam,
      The Queer Art of Failure, p. 88.

The hardest, yet most valuable challenge I have been facing in my quest for embodied theory is the recognition of the need to articulate, in form and content, my own position as a highly privileged white European intellectual who engages with the embodied realities of marginalized people's bodies, while also experiencing my own body as ambivalently confirming yet resisting normative cultural expectations. For my own writing, I will thus rehearse what Jack Halberstam and Tavia Nyong'o call *Wild Theory* with the goal of becoming more sensitive to the hitherto neglected aspects in the processes of writing visual theory: "In theory [...] the wild need not be delimited by its uses within a colonial, antiblack lexicon. Nor is it exhausted by the romantic image of spontaneous revolt. Wild Theory uses and abuses these lexicons and brutal grammars while extending them, amplifying them, contesting some and ignoring others."[30] My hope is to become more responsive, attentive to what we commonly fail to smell, sense, feel, or hear from bodies.

> The absence of some bodies in representation can thus possibly be compensated by a different reading of visual content: a reading that considers the fact that in an image of something might be present, yet invisible. The absence of certain forms of visibility is, as we have seen, not so much, or not only, a problem of image-making but of image-reading.[31]

I will be mindful to ask myself more often, "So now that you can't see me, will you hear me better?"[32]

30   Jack Halberstam and Tavia Nyong'o, "Introduction: Theory in the Wild,"
        South Atlantic Quarterly, vol. 117, no. 3 (2018), pp. 453-64, here p. 455.
31   Sturm, *Bodies We Fail*, pp. 147-48.
32   Nduwanje, "DO NOT READ THIS BODY"

A Case for the Abolition of Men

One evening, six weeks after I was punched twice to the ground by a stranger as I walked home, I found myself too anxious to face the stares and/or verbal harassment that usually greets my entry into public space. Luckily, my community had raised funds to help me in such a situation and I ordered a delivery rather than going to get my dinner myself. As I sat down to eat it, chewing gingerly to avoid aggravating the slowly healing fracture in my jaw, I was startled by a loud banging in my building. My first thought was that someone was trying to break into my apartment and I experienced a dizzyingly vivid vision of a Man walking into my kitchen and attacking me. But this was only a vision. It turned out that a Man on the floor below me was trying to get into an apartment. He was ringing the doorbell repeatedly and banging on the door with intense violence, yelling in a language that I didn't understand or recognize. I was paralyzed. I had no idea what I should do. After I was attacked, the police were surprisingly kind. But I am white. I didn't know anything about this Man beyond that he was inducing a panic response in me and he wasn't yelling in German or English. I didn't know what the police would do to him if they came. I sat breathing shallowly with my heart racing, feeling outside my body, and watching supposedly solid surfaces in my kitchen begin to undulate and pulse. I sat there like this for around forty minutes until the police arrived. Someone else had called them. I peeked downstairs and the Man screaming and smashing at the door was my neighbor, a kind-seeming Man who I'm pretty sure lives alone. He works around the house and we always say hello when we walk past each other. He was extremely drunk and couldn't work out how to get into his own apartment. As my breathing slowly returned to normal and the life came back into my limbs it became clear to me that Men must be abolished.

> *One of my earliest memories is of two boys in the first year of school tying a skipping rope around my neck and pulling it so tight that I couldn't breathe. I don't remember how or why they stopped, but they must have because I am still alive.*

Men are a problem. A problem that refuses to solve itself. Over decades, women, femmes, butches, drag queens and kings, nonbinary

people, genderqueers, and many others have been grappling with
what to do with this profoundly dysfunctional group of people. They
are everywhere, dominating almost every sphere of society and
anxiously penetrating into those they don't. Feminist activism and
thought has developed a wealth of strategies and paradigms to con-
tribute to the building of a world that isn't structured around male
dominance and impunity. Non-Men have labored passionately at
creating new ways of gendered being. People have given their lives
the world over to make this change. And this whole time, Men have
remained static, immobile, stubborn, selfish, willfully stupid, and,
worst of all, omnipresent.

It is obvious that Men must be abolished. However, even if we
accept the self-evident truth that Men must be entirely done away
with (rather than simply reformed), it is still necessary to work out
the strengths and weaknesses of this argument. I will use the writing
of others to support what can only be a collective task. The abolition
of Men must be accomplished by a broad coalition. Yet, in relying
on the writing of others, it is important not to forget that this text is
the result of my embodied experience. I believe that only a body that
has my unique experiences could have written this and then, if this is
true, the same must be true of each of the writers to which I refer in
this chapter. This is something to keep in mind as we approach these
various perspectives.

Men. A Stubborn Problem.

Perhaps one of the most inspiring and impactful voices on this unfor-
tunate topic (Men) is Valerie Solanas. Her groundbreaking *S.C.U.M.
Manifesto*, originally self-published and distributed in 1967 in New
York, offers an invaluable insight into the problems of Men.

> *A friend of mine used to have an apartment with a window that
> you could climb out of to get on the roof of the building next door.
> We had an after-party up there and, as we sat, pupils dilating
> to take in the outrageously camp spectacle of the sunrise, the
> harassment and abuse that I had experienced at school came up.
> I don't remember it so well because we were all on ecstasy and
> it didn't feel significant at the time. Years later, a woman who
> was there told me that her friend, a guy whose face I already then*

couldn't remember, had told her afterwards that I must have
been making some of it up and that it was inappropriate to make
such a big deal of it: "It can't have been that bad." I don't recall
making such a big deal of it. It still doesn't feel like such a big deal.
It's my life. A collection of things that I have experienced. But
"nice" Men are often very shocked when you tell them the things
that other Men do. It is a performance with a beginning, a middle,
and, most importantly, an end; at which point it is no longer
appropriate to dwell on it. In this case, I had failed to notice the
expiration date of my pain. I was genuinely embarrassed. How
self-indulgent of me.

Solanas sees through the veneer of male virility to its fragile core:
"Although he wants to be an individual, the male is scared of anything
in himself that is the slightest bit different from other men, it causes
him to suspect that he's not really a 'Man,' that he's passive and totally
sexual, a highly upsetting suspicion. If other men are 'A' and he's not,
he must not be a man, he must be a fag. So he tries to affirm his 'Manhood' by being like all the other men. Differentness in other men, as
well as himself, threatens him; it means they're fags whom he must at
all costs avoid, so he tries to make sure that all other men conform."[1]
Here, Solanas points to a key element of Man-ness: conformity. There
is so much at stake in being a Man that difference becomes deadly.
My own experience backs up Solanas' theory. I am mostly perceived
by Men as a man who has, through some foul act of gender treachery,
allowed himself to degenerate into an un-man; a fag. This makes me
useful, though: a prop. You learn the particular look in the eye of a boy
or a Man who has marked you and will use you to perform his masculine conformity by spitting, yelling, hitting, or otherwise punishing
you for allowing yourself to slide, limp-wristed and weak, through the
iron bars of masculine conformity. This frantic self-regulation doesn't
just play out inside the Man-subject. In fact, it must always be played
out on others. "To be sure he's a 'Man,' the male must see to it that
the female be clearly a 'Woman,' the opposite of a 'Man,' that is, the
female must act like a faggot."[2] Men are very concerned with how

---

1   Valerie Solanas, *S.C.U.M. Manifesto (Society for Cutting up Men)*, 1967,
     n.p. http://kunsthallezurich.ch/sites/default/files/scum_manifesto.pdf.
2   Ibid.

others act, because it is the only metric by which they can continue
to believe that they are, in fact, still Men. When a Man spits at me, or
someone like me, in fact he is anxiously checking the pulse of his own
heterosexual Manhood. Still there? Thank God.

So that's heterosexual Men. What about the gays? If the same
violent conformity oppresses gay Men as it does women, is there
some natural affinity upon which one could build a resistance? Well,
it depends on the material and social conditions. Over the years since
Solanas wrote *S.C.U.M. Manifesto,* many (middle-class, white) gay
Men have enjoyed a remarkable improvement in their social stand-
ing. However, Solanas' prescience shines a clarifying light through
the intervening decades even to Berlin in 2020: "in addition to
engaging in the time honored and classical wars and race riots, men
are more and more either becoming fags or are obliterating themselves through drugs."[3] It is a sad fact that gay Men have enjoyed the
lion's share of the hard-won gains of the gay liberation movement
that was spearheaded by Black and Brown drag queens and trans
people and they spend this newfound freedom obliterating themselves in clubs, taking up space and resources, while appropriating the
language of liberation to describe the specific neurochemical effects
of ketamine. They either idolize (dehumanize) the trans femmes and
drag queens who birthed their culture, or they revile them. Cisgender women, who played midwife to many of these Men's burgeoning
gay identities, are pushed to the margins. Gay Men appropriate the
various hypermasculine aesthetics of earlier fetish scenes—forget-
ting the irony involved in their creation—and have created a new cult
of masculinity centered around a phallus that is so intoxicated it is
unable to maintain an erection.

> *In the seventh year of school, a boy bubbling anxiously on the cusp*
> *of Manhood followed me around the schoolyard taunting me*
> *by performatively speculating on my (deviant) sexuality. After*
> *a while, I turned around and asked him "Doesn't it seem a*
> *bit confused that you're accusing me of being gay when you're the*
> *one that's following me around? It kind of seems like you're the*
> *one that loves me." A hushed silence. An older boy, further along*
> *in his transition into Manhood, prompted my tormentor "Are*

3   Ibid.

*you going to just take that?" I could see it dawning on him that
he was now called upon to prove himself. He walked up close to
me, pupils wide, and said in a low, grating voice "You're going to
regret that you fucking faggot" and began to punch me in the
stomach. I maintained eye contact with him, passively accepting
the blows to my body. This denied him his cue as to when to stop,
so after a while he said in a half-defeated tone, "That's what you
get." He was right. It was what I got. A fellow student forced me
to take this to the (male) school principal who then pulled the boy
into his office and spoke to him. I was called in shortly after
and informed that I was also to apologize. It was made clear to
me that even though the other boy had to come 90 percent of the
way, it was me that had to make up the other 10 percent. I was
only beginning to feel the physical pain of the attack. It was all
in my stomach, but my arms and hands were fine because I had
not attempted to defend myself. I apologized for receiving the
attack. Later that year my best friend grabbed me in a headlock
from behind and rammed my head into the corner of a brick wall
because I said something that annoyed him. I needed three
stitches. It was what I got.*

All this begs the question: Where on earth does this problem come
from? The answer is that they are made. One is not born a Man, but
rather he becomes one. In her 2004 book, *The Will to Change*, bell
hooks describes the process by which boys (those assigned male at
birth) are brutalized into Men: "Patriarchal assault on the emotional
life of boys begins at the moment of their birth."[4] From there onwards,
"patriarchal culture requires that boys deny, suppress, and if all goes
well, shut down their emotional awareness and their capacity to feel.
Little boys are the only males in our culture who are allowed to be
fully, wholly in touch with their feelings, allowed moments when
they can express without shame their desire to love and be loved. If
they are very, very lucky, they are able to remain connected to their
inner selves or some part of their inner selves before they enter a
patriarchal school system where rigid sex roles will be enforced as

4   bell hooks, *The Will to Change: Men, Masculinity, and Love.* New York:
     Washington Square Press, 2004, p. 35.

rigorously as they are in any male prison."[5] hooks also questions the commonly accepted social and emotional withdrawal of teenage boys as they enter their cocoon stage of masculinity, arguing that this commonly accepted facet of male maturation is, in fact, a sign of pathology and dissociation. The only acceptable emotion left to boys and young Men becomes anger and "eruptions of rage in boys are most often deemed normal, explained by the age old justification 'boys will be boys.'"[6] Given that we are surrounded by the products of this violent baptism of masculinist fire, is it any wonder that we find ourselves in such a predicament?

(Not) All Men.

One morning I was riding my bike to the physiotherapist to receive a jaw massage. Since I had my jaw broken, I clench my teeth in the night and I experience painful cramps during the day. So, I obtained a prescription for physiotherapy from my orthopedist and made an appointment. My nervous system was aflame, alert to the slightest indication of danger. Every other bike or car on the road was a potential threat and I was frantically trying to keep track of each of them. This was partly because I had just started riding again after a three-year hiatus and partly because this is what I now do with other bodies in public space. It feels a bit like juggling chainsaws. In this hyperalert, agitated state, I was focusing on the need to remain calm but aware enough to continue riding. To do this I was taking long deep breaths, focusing on the exhale. Suddenly I was overtaken by a shock. A Man in a fast-moving ton of steel, rubber, and plastic was veering towards me shrieking words I couldn't understand. I panicked. Time sped up and slowed down at the same time. My skin felt tight. I didn't know why he was doing this to me. I may have run a red light or committed some other minor traffic violation. I don't know. I was only conscious that a Man in a car was overtaking me, screaming at me in too-fast, too-loud German about some real or imagined infraction that I had committed in order to teach me a lesson. Men have a lot of things they want to teach people.

5   Ibid., pp. 41–42.
6   Ibid., 51.

I was focused too much on not crashing my bike to learn the lesson.
It took me the rest of the ride to calm my breathing again.

Now we've acknowledged that we have a problem. Good. That's the
first step. But admitting that there is an urgent crisis at the heart of
society is not the same as understanding its nature. When we consider the problem of Men historically, we can see that it is in many
cases more complicated than our anecdotal evidence (which nearly
always leads us to the conclusion that Men are garbage) may lead
us to believe. In describing the history of struggles against racial
and sexual oppression in the United States, Angela Davis outlines
how two of the staunchest supporters of women's suffrage (Frederick Douglass and W. E. B. Dubois) were, in fact, not women.[7] In
addition, women were welcomed at the 1869 founding convention
of the National Colored Labor Union by Black workers who wanted
to avoid "the mistakes heretofore made by our white fellow citizens
in omitting women."[8] To complicate matters further, in fact, it was
the women's suffrage movement (dominated by white, middle-class
women) that frequently acted against the interests of Black women
(and men) throughout the nineteenth and early twentieth centuries.
Davis points out that this same movement frequently worked against
the interests of working-class women, with Susan B. Anthony encour-
aging women to perform scab labor, which harmed the interests of
all working people. This attitude can be most clearly observed in her
statement that "an oligarchy of wealth, where the rich govern the poor;
an oligarchy of learning; where the educated govern the ignorant; or
even an oligarchy of race, where the Saxon rules the African, might
be endured; but this oligarchy of sex which makes father, brothers,
husband, sons, the oligarchs over the mother and the sisters, the wife
and daughters of every household; which ordains all men sovereigns,
all women subjects—carries discord and rebellion into every home
of the nation."[9] Anthony's shocking capacity to allow economic and
racial domination in the name of fighting against sexism is, argues
Davis, "a staunch reflection of bourgeois ideology. And it was proba-
bly because of the ideology's blinding powers that she failed to realize

7   Angela Davis, *Women, Race and Class.* New York: Vintage Books, 1983.
8   Ibid., p. 138.
9   Susan B. Anthony quoted from Davis, ibid., p. 142.

that working-class women and Black women alike were fundamentally linked to their men by the class exploitation and racist oppression which did not discriminate between the sexes."[10] So, we have here another problem. According to the history related by Davis, it is not infrequently white, middle-class women who are perpetuating the suffering of (Black and working) women, while (Black) men are showing remarkable solidarity with the struggle of all women.

This contradiction (like most interesting contradictions) can only be resolved with a radical departure from essentialism. In her recent book *Females*, Andrea Long Chu, inspired by Valerie Solanas herself, proposes: "a universal sex defined by self-negation, against which all politics, even feminist politics, rebels."[11] This sex, of course, is the female. Chu is not arguing that every single person is biologically female. She writes that when "I talk about females, I am not referring to biological sex, though I'm not referring to gender either. I'm referring instead to something that might as well be sex, the way that reactionaries describe it [...] but whose nature is ontological, not biological."[12] Inside this framework, there is room for gender difference—in fact, the specific way in which one deals with one's femaleness is what gives rise to one's gender. At the root of this femaleness is the way one exists in the world. Chu defines as female "any psychic operation in which the self is sacrificed to make room for the desires of another."[13]

> *I passed a Man on a street corner recently. He was absentmindedly tossing a glass bottle into the air and catching it. As I came closer, I experienced an extremely vivid vision of him catching the bottle, neck first, and using it to bludgeon my skull. This vision was so intense I lost contact with my surroundings, but I was vaguely aware that I was trying not to visibly flinch from him. Trembling, I forced myself to look back at him. He hadn't noticed me passing. It occurred to me that this is not normal.*

Into Chu's framework I propose Men as a subset of these "females" who are defined by their incapacity to stop their own internal suffering

10   Ibid.
11   Andrea Long Chu, *Females*. London: Verso, 2019, p. 11.
12   Ibid., p. 12.
13   Ibid., p. 11.

from spilling over and harming others. A Man is any person who is consistently unable to have a problem without turning it into the much bigger problem of another person or group of people. Everyone is female, but only some of us are Men. And they're a problem. Susan B. Anthony, in her willingness to sacrifice Black and working-class women (and men) in her pursuit of women's suffrage, was a Man. Frederick Douglass and W. E. B. Dubois, in their consistent solidarity with the feminist cause, were not.

I am not proposing this category as an ahistorical phenomenon. Following socialist feminists such as Silvia Federici, Nancy Fraser, Bini Adamczak, and Angela Davis, I believe it is possible to trace Men back to a particular social formation that arose at the time of the Industrial Revolution. They are a product of the Western European bourgeois imaginary and their ways have spread, like a virus, throughout the world, via capitalist exploitation and colonial conquest and domination.

On June 10, 2020, as protests against police brutality and systemic racism ignited across the US and many other parts of the world, popular children's author and renowned Man, J. K. Rowling, published a 3,680-word blog post in which he portrayed himself as a victim of persecution by the transgender lobby. This post referred to various (uncited) sources in order to build the case that (cisgender) women are endangered by the intrusion of trans people into "their" spaces. Rowling sketched a vision of a society in which women are threatened by a pandemic of violence conducted by Men dressed up as women. There is no such pandemic. There is no evidence of this occurring. There is, however, a crushingly large body of evidence showing that trans people, in particular trans women, in particular trans women of color, are being murdered at hugely disproportionate rates. This fact should be obvious to anyone with an internet connection. It is apparently lost on Rowling. Interestingly, the only violence conducted by a Man who is dressed up as a woman in this situation is that perpetrated by the author himself.

otherwise

What Is To Be Done (With Men)?

Given what we know about Men, we are confronted with the question: What on earth are we going to do about them? The simplest, perhaps the most satisfying answer, unsurprisingly, is found in Solanas' *Manifesto*: kill them. "It doesn't follow that the male, like disease, has always existed among us that he should continue to exist."[14] In one sense, the logic here is undeniable. The problem arises, however, when one is confronted with the task of working out just who exactly is a Man. As noted above, one cannot simply look at a person and tell whether they are or are not a Man. Man-ness is a way of being in the world. It is a way of relating to others. Rooting out all Men would be logistically impossible, and the violence of doing away with them would pose a very real threat of turning us all into Men ourselves. If the existence of Men is our problem and by solving that problem we make it their problem, we end up as freshly minted Men. Unfortunately, killing all Men just wouldn't be practicable.

> *Once I got to the physiotherapist, and as I lay down on the table it struck me that he had a similar frame and heavy masculine presence to the Man who attacked me. As his large, skilled hands massaged my jaw, I found myself wondering how these two Men could have such different effects on my body. I suddenly found it very hard not to cry.*

Another option would be individual self-reconstruction. Men could be encouraged to take the initiative to change themselves into something less socially destructive. One might expect that given my life experience, I believe that individual Men should drop their current identities and shift their gendered practices in the trans femme direction, but I can't say I'd recommend it. It's very difficult, the harassment and assault is relentless, and I wouldn't wish the behavior of Men on anyone, not even Men.

Fortunately, Solanas offers another hint. "After the elimination of money there will be no further need to kill men, they will be stripped of the only power they have over psychologically independent females."[15]

14   Solanas, *S.C.U.M. Manifesto*.
15   Ibid.

In fact, money is a key tool in the enforcement of male power: "Having an obsessive desire to be admired by women, but no intrinsic worth, the male constructs a highly artificial society enabling him to appropriate the appearance of worth through money, prestige, 'high' social class, degrees, professional position and knowledge and, by pushing as many other men as possible down professionally, socially, economically and educationally."[16] Thus, if Men are the result of a specific set of power relations then perhaps the key lies in changing these preconditions.

We find a necessary precondition for men in capitalism. Where some feminist theorists have argued that capitalism is one aspect or manifestation of millennia of patriarchal rule of women, others (such as Davis) have instead emphasized the role of this totalizing system in constructing the gendered matrixes in which we live. Karl Marx points to the way that estranged labor perverts the existence of humankind: "In estranging from man (1) nature, and (2) himself, his own active functions, his life activity, estranged labour estranges the *species* from man. It changes for him the *life of the species* into a means of individual life. First it estranges the life of the species and individual life, and secondly it makes individual life in its abstract form the purpose of the life of the species, likewise in its abstract and estranged form."[17] It is the process of estrangement, whereby the human being is alienated from their surroundings and even their species, which creates Men. Rather than being an integrated member of a species that works towards harmony with their surroundings, Man under capitalism believes that the species and all of nature exists to further his own interests. This fetish of the individual, which reverses and confuses the relations between humans, is a key element in the perpetuation and proliferation of Men. Therefore, it follows that any serious attempt to abolish them would require the radical restructuring of the preconditions for their existence. If Men are a result of human estrangement from their species and all non-human nature, this estrangement, and the capitalist system that produces it, must be ended. It turns out that the problem of Men, like most interesting problems, can only be solved "durch den

16   Ibid.
17   Karl Marx, "Estranged Labour," *Economic and Philosophical Manuscripts of 1844*, 2009 [1932], trans. Martin Milligan https://www.marxists.org /archive/marx/works/1844/manuscripts/labour.htm, accessed July 13, 2020.

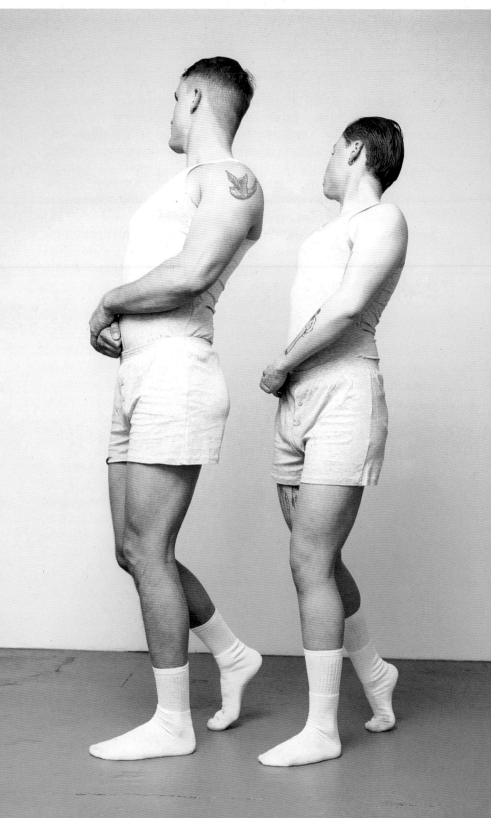

gewaltsamen Umsturz aller bisherigen Gesellschaftsordnung."[18]
Following Marx's argument, Nancy Fraser, in conversation with
Rahel Jaeggi, argues: "genuine self-determination requires both
personal and collective freedom. The two are internally connected.
Neither can be assured in the absence of the other."[19] The human, in
order to be free, must be reunited with their self as a species-being
in relation to non-human nature. In other words, they must lean into
their femaleness. Chu's argument that all politics rebels against the
human's inherent femaleness rests upon a presupposition of a liberal
mode of politics that fetishizes the individual. The interests of others,
which she casts as an imposition upon individual will, need not be
perceived as something that lies in contradiction to the interests of
the self. Rediscovering our capacity for species-being (embracing our
femaleness) allows us to cease rebelling against the needs of others as
though they are an oppressive external force, and to see instead the
inherently relational nature of our being. Everyone is indeed female,
but not everyone hates it. Some of us love it.

> On Sunday April 12 at 23:40, a friend of mine was walking me
> home from her house. We had watched the Seventh Seal because
> I'd been told a number of times that I resemble Death in it. As
> it turns out, I kind of do, but I think that's mostly because I wear
> all black and talk about depression a lot. We had drunk a bottle
> of wine while watching the film. As we walked along Richardstraße
> two Men passed us. I didn't hear the exchange but one of the
> Men had asked my friend if we were gay. She replied "Yes, and?"
> We kept walking and I asked my friend what he had said. She
> told me, and I replied, "Ugh fuck, I hate Men" and looked back.
> He had turned around and was following us, arms swinging
> ominously at his sides. I remember looking around on the ground

18   Karl Marx and Friedrich Engels, *Manifest der Kommunistischen Partei.*
      London: Communist League, 1848, p. 23, see http://www.deutsches
      textarchiv.de/book/view/marx_manifestws_1848?p=23, accessed
      October 2, 2020. Engl. trans. Samuel Moore, 2004: "by the forcible
      overthrow of all existing social conditions," see https://www.marxists
      .org/archive/marx/works/1848/communist-manifesto/ch04.htm,
      accessed October 21, 2020.
19   Nancy Fraser and Rahel Jaeggi, *Capitalism: A Conversation in Critical
      Theory,* (ed.) Brian Milstein. Cambridge, MA: Polity Press, 2018, p. 131.

for a bottle. Bottles can be very useful. Usually if I'm already holding one I subtly change my grip so that I can wield it more effectively. I've lived in Berlin for eight years, so I should have known that it was extremely unlikely that there would be a stray Pfandflasche *lying around, but I guess I wasn't thinking straight. A couple of times in the past, when there hasn't been a bottle around, I've slipped off a stiletto and gripped that in my hand. The concentration of all that force on such a small point can inflict quite a lot of pain, so it can be a handy tool for self-defense. But I was wearing flats. He caught up with us at Alfred-Scholz-Platz. There were not so many people around because the lockdown was still in place. He began to interrogate us, asking us again if we were gay, and whether we were together. My friend answered that yes, we were gay, and no we were not together. I was suddenly infuriated at the situation. I Interrupted and said, "What you are doing is totally unacceptable. You are following two strangers down the street at night and interrogating them about their sexuality for no reason. It is totally out of control and you need to leave us alone." He tried to say something and I interrupted again and said, "No, you don't need to say anything, you just need to leave us alone. Just fuck off. Go." He answered me by punching me twice in the jaw. I crumpled to the ground both times. I stood up both times just as quickly. I'm proud of that. His friend had caught up with him and pulled him away before he could hit me a third time. My mouth was suddenly full and wet. I spat onto the ground and it was a gorgeous dark red. With the first punch, he broke my jaw. This required surgery, which has healed now, although I was unable to chew for six weeks, and I am waiting to regain feeling on the lower right-hand side of my face. People can't really notice, but my smile is lopsided now. When I go on dates, I wonder whether it's better to explain why my face looks this way or just pretend it's not demanding my full attention. I fell onto a pile of stacked chairs and bruised my elbow badly. This required a cast. I am still undergoing physiotherapy for this. The second punch was less intense; I don't know why. I only got a cut on my jaw from that one and it healed quickly, but did leave a scar, which I don't like. My body is lined with the traces of this Man's touch. It will be for a long time.*

So then, we find that the solution to the problem of Men is only really in the overthrow of the economic, social, and political preconditions that perpetuate their unfortunate proliferation. Among the various aims of the movement(s) that will carry out this revolutionary process must be the abolition of Men. Because, just as Men are a product of an unjust and inhumane system, they are also one of our biggest impediments to real change being made. Thus, as society is remade, so too must our ways of being together change in such a way that Men are not possible. In her analysis of the problems of the October 1917 Russian Revolution, Bini Adamczak writes "Die historischen Geschlechter samt der sie hervorbringenden Beziehungsweisen und der von ihnen hervorgebrachten Existenzweisen müssten dafür als gewordener Speicher affektiver, habitueller, intellektueller, praktischer Reichtümer verstanden werden, aus denen eine Gesellschaft im Prozess ihrer Befreiung wählen kann."[20] Adamczak is right, and her critical approach to gender and its role in social liberation is urgently necessary, although I would add that we need to be discerning in the choices we make. We can and should look forward to a time when Men are a thing of the past. They have nothing to offer the future except their absence.

---

20   Bini Adamczak, *Beziehungsweise Revolution: 1917, 1968 und kommende.* Berlin: Suhrkamp, 2018, p.174. Engl. trans.: "The historical genders, including the relationships that create them and the modes of existence that they create, would have to be understood as a repository of affective, habitual, intellectual, practical riches from which a society can choose in the process of its liberation."

Bodies on the Outside

Artistic Imagination
in Afrofuturism

> "Redressing the pained body encompasses operating in and
> against the demands of the system, negotiating the disci-
> plinary harnessing of the body, and counterinvesting in the
> body as a site of possibility."
> —Saidiya Hartman, *Scenes of Subjection*

We often only become aware of our body when it lets us down, when
we cannot keep it under control or we bump into something—in other
words, when we find our own body difficult to read. And we only notice
other bodies when they are different, when we idealize or desire them,
or when we find them repulsive.

For people with experiences of migration and/or racism, the
body—their body—is an unavoidable issue. Often enough, their body
is the bone of contention. When we are reflecting on the subject of the
body, therefore, it is important to take our own experiences as our
point of departure. How is our body being read? When does it emerge
from the background, or indeed become the most important topic?
When does our own body feel vulnerable? Do bodies only become
visible when they are marked as different, when they are suffering
and vulnerable? What potential does the body offer us? How can marginalized positions be made productive, and what opportunities for
new images are created when we outline the pitfalls involved? These
are key issues that frame theoretical reflections on racism, bodies,
and alternative readings of the body.

On these premises the bildungsLab* was founded in 2017.[1] The
basic idea was simple: Female* academics of color and/or with migration histories who work in the fields of arts and sciences share their
everyday experiences of discrimination, practices of resistance, and
research findings by discussing them, writing about them, and using

1   As members of the bildungsLab*, the authors (with Lalitha Chamakalayil
     and Shadi Kooroshy) developed and led a workshop on "Körper-Alpha-
     betisierungen [Body literacy]: Corpoliteracy in Educational and Cultural
     Institutions," on September 15, 2019, which formed part of the sympo-
     sium *Reading bodies!* (2019) at HKW.

them productively in theoretical and practical contexts. Given suffi-
cient scope, these kinds of experiences can enable *other* forms of
knowledge production. They reveal the extent to which power is exer-
cised through the gaze, how forms of institutional or structural exclusion affect subjects, and how new subjects and collectivities develop.
The aim here is to incorporate personal experiences of, and reflections on, marginalization and stigmatization into theoretical and
practical investigations. This approach is not about navel-gazing or
fostering a narcissistic self, but instead serves the purpose of herme-
neutic location: determining when, where, and how these moments
of marginalization occur and put us in a particular position, and what
subversive forms of opposition or resistance are to be found in our
personal, collective, and historical repertoire. The chosen method
requires a discursive space where participants neither have to fight
discrimination, nor do they have to accept the ambivalent offer of a
token position. To this end, we are working on creating a library of
counterintuitive ideas on education and art.[2]

In her book *Notes Toward a Performative Theory of Assembly*
(2015), Judith Butler describes the body as being "exposed, to history,
to precarity, and to force, but also to what is unbidden and felicitous,
like passion and love, or sudden friendship or sudden or unexpected
loss."[3] How bodies are perceived and judged depends on a number
of factors. A person's body can be a source of regulation, shame, and
happiness at one and the same time. Bodies are a constant reminder
of the precariousness of life. They often become entangled in a relationship of dependency on the *other*, as well as in a capitalist system
of exploitation and exclusion. Being aware of and acknowledging this
fragility is a necessary condition for ethical practice.

If we consider our own biography, we can see that it represents
an accumulation of bodily (re-)actions, as well as reactions to the reactions of *others* to our bodies. Affects have a history. Who is subjected to violence, and how often, because the very presence of their
body generates hatred and/or fear? Who gains recognition simply because their body is considered pleasing and attractive? What

2   These ideas and concepts are explored in a series of books entitled
      "Resistance & Desire," published by Zaglossus Verlag in Vienna. The first
      volume, *Bildung. Ein postkoloniales Manifest*, is currently in press.
3   Judith Butler, *Notes Toward a Performative Theory of Assembly*. Cambridge,
      MA: Harvard University Press, 2015, p.148.

traumas cause the body to freeze? What traumas set it in motion? And above all: What fuels utopian visions of overcoming violence or trauma?

Bodies are neither material objects nor subjects per se, but are instead constantly developing and changing. They are situated in a history of fetishization, alienation, attraction, and shaming. People are shamed whose bodies do not conform to hegemonic notions of normality: in Europe and the United States, for example, they are shamed if their bodies are not white; if they are unable to walk unaided or have other visible physical limitations; if they do not desire the opposite sex in accordance with the heterosexual matrix; if they refuse to be categorized as male or female; or if they use sign language rather than speech or sounds as a means of communication. A recognition of one goes hand in hand with a rejection of the *other*.

These phenomena appear the world over albeit in different forms. Here, however, the focus is on those bodies which most of Europe is reluctant to consider as an integral part of the civic community: bodies which—in the process of racialization—have been categorized as non-normal. In this context, racism can be described as a violent reading of the body, a process whereby the chances of remaining unharmed and leading a happy life are unequally distributed. This text is therefore explicitly intended as a critique of racializing productions of the body and, as it were, a statement on the (im-) possibility of moving beyond racist imaginations.

On Being Seen

Bodies are abstracted, classified, (over)determined, judged, and constructed through the gaze of others. Reading and classifying the body involves hegemonic practices; these help to reinforce categorizations and imaginations that are themselves permeated by social structures and power relations. Bodies are thus made into racialized, sexualized, *other* bodies. In *Ways of Seeing* (1972), John Berger writes that even though seeing comes before words, we have to learn how to see; he notes that looking always involves choosing and situating things in relation to one another. These observations are helpful when it comes to thinking about the invisibility of bodies. On the relationship between seeing and being seen, for example, Berger writes: "The eye of the other combines with our own eye to make it fully credible that we are part of the visible world."[4]

In *Black Skin, White Masks* (1952), Frantz Fanon defines the dialectical relationship in the white gaze upon black people as the erasure of a self, a process in which the experience of being seen is articulated, but the ontology of self-consciousness is not completed. He regards the phantasmatic fixation by the white gaze rather as an existential feeling of not being able to escape—a "zone of nonbeing."[5] The American movement of thought known as Afro-pessimism (Saidiya Hartman) describes everyday scenes of Black life and social death in an anti-Black world. Many leading thinkers such as Frank B. Wilderson III, Jared Sexton, Orlando Patterson, Katherine McKittrick, and Christina Sharpe have examined the process of becoming Black and the production of Black bodies against the background of the transatlantic slave trade. The poet Fred Moten, on the other hand, argues that moments of improvisation and resistance can also be found in an apocalyptic present. In his book *Stolen Life* (2018), Moten emphasizes that the power of transformation, and likewise the power of blackness, lies in fugitivity:

Fugitivity, then, is a desire for and a spirit of escape and transgression of the proper and the proposed. It's a desire for the outside, for a playing or being outside, an outlaw edge proper to the now always already improper voice or instrument.[6]

For Moten, along the lines of Hartman, Blackness means being situated on the outside, but it nevertheless exerts a productive force through fugitivity, transgression, and escape—through flight. It means Black bodies and screams that refuse to be contained, that fall silent and escape. However, it is also the traumatic experiences of dispossession, theft, and enslavement that constitute the desire for the outside. Recognizing the overdetermination of bodies makes it possible to identify the processes that produce them. These processes, in turn, have the potential to deviate from this normative pattern.

4   John Berger, *Ways of Seeing*. London: Penguin Books, 1972, p. 9.
5   Frantz Fanon, *Black Skin, White Masks*, trans. Richard Philcox. New York, NY: Grove Press, 2008, p. xii.
6   Fred Moten, *Stolen Life (consent not to be a single being)*. Durham, NC: Duke University Press, 2018, p. 131.

"Space is the Place":
Bodies in Afrofuturism,
Affects, and Cyborgs

How could the idea of liberation from the body, from representations of the body, be taken a step further? It is no coincidence that we find answers to this question in the genre of science fiction and in Afrofuturism, where the imagination is transported to utopian realms and/or outer space. This involves reinventing the self and consequently emancipating the body, along with modes of thinking, from the current structures. Afrofuturism focuses on the past and present, but also on future conceptions, from an African-American/Black perspective that is mediated through speculative futurism and technoculture aesthetics.[7] Afrofuturism proposes "histories of counter-futures."[8] These counter-drafts raise questions as to how we deal with temporality, conceptions of the human, and the Anthropocene epoch. The science fiction and fantasy genres have been decisively influenced, for example, by the Afrofuturist works of Octavia Butler, Samuel R. Delany, and Tananarive Due (as well as numerous other writers). They not only address issues of representation, but also call into question the category of "the human" and liberal concepts of humanism. Why do we distinguish ourselves from animals, vampires, cyborgs, and hybrids? What new connections are generated by new (bio-)technologies, superpowers, and other essential forms? Ideas on the liberation of bodies can often be found not only in future realms, but also in current technology and in the transformation of functional objects and physical abilities (e.g. such as the superhuman abilities of characters from comic books like Wonder Woman, Wolverine, Spider-Man, Black Panther, and Shuri).

The Afrofuturist movement was both firmly rooted in and far ahead of its time. In the twenty-first century, and above all in the face of the coronavirus pandemic of 2020, the climate crisis, and the rise of populist movements that essentially propagate autocratic values, the

---

7   Mark Dery, *Flame Wars: The Discourse of Cyberculture*. Durham, NC: Duke
     University Press, 1994, p. 180.
8   Kodwo Eshun, quoted from Susana M. Morris, "Black Girls Are from the
     Future: Afrofuturist Feminism in Octavia E. Butler's 'Fledgling,'"
     Women's Studies Quarterly, vol. 40, nos 3/4 (2012), pp. 146–66, here p. 153
     http://www.jstor.org/stable/23333483, accessed October 14, 2020.

motifs of an Afrofuturist world seem to be in discursive harmony with a desire to escape from the material present. In the galactic cult film *Space is the Place* (1974), for example, the influential jazz musician Sun Ra presents a future for an African-American population (starting with Black people from Oakland, California) on a new planet in outer space. Via the medium of music, the people invited to inhabit his new cosmos are transported to a spaceship, which then takes them to the new planet. This and many other examples show that visions of future are not a workshop where "reparations" are made or something broken is restored, but that real power lies in creating alternative worlds and magical, tech-based bodies.

What if Sun Ra was right, and space really is the place? Sun Ra outlined his utopian conception of Afrofuturism—a Black future—in his music and visual media in the 1960s, and as early as 1903, Pauline Hopkins wrote one of the first prototypical Afrofuturist novels, entitled *Of One Blood: Or, The Hidden Self*.[9] In 2018, the return of Afrofuturism was celebrated in the globally successful Hollywood movie *Black Panther*. Around the same time, the music industry also began to embrace the movement; artists such as Janelle Monáe (with her music video *Dirty Computer* in 2018) and Jay-Z (with his video for *Family Feud* in 2017), for example, presented visions of a technology-driven world ruled by queer Black women.

These productions play with the aesthetics of technology and origin, creating positive images of numerous African societies and new diversities. In particular, they enable us to imagine a place "untouched by colonialism." The idea of outer space, the moon and stars, as an alternative location gave many protagonists in the Afrofuturist movement an opportunity to step outside a world in which they were physically trapped. As Jacques Derrida wrote in 1995, an archive is constituted only through its "outside."[10] Similarly, Moten's proposal of "blackness as fugitivity" shows us that many productive projections of the body are developed and "counter-futures" are conceived by playing with the notions of "outside," "beyond," and "outer space."

---

9   Pauline Hopkins, "Of One Blood: Or, the Hidden Self," serialized in *The Colored American Magazine*, vols 5–6 (1902–03).

10 Jacques Derrida, "Archive Fever: A Freudian Impression," trans. Eric Prenowitz, *Diacritics*, vol. 25, no. 2 (1995), pp. 9–63, here p. 14.

The School of Seeing and the Art
of Expanding an Atrophied Imagination

Afrofuturist images, sound worlds, and narratives can be described as attempts to erase hegemonic codes and imagine deracialized markers and different social systems beyond capitalist, neoliberal, patriarchal, and racist structures. The acts of seeing and reading the body are thereby exposed as powerful tools of subjugation. If, however, the *other* is conceived by the *others* themselves, this can generate alternative modes of seeing and reading that have enduring relevance. In a way, Afrofuturist spaces counterpoint those we are currently experiencing in all their cruelty: spaces where we are being suffocated by a racist-humanist triumphalism; spaces whose fragility becomes apparent in the face of a pandemic that once again reminds us we are not "all in the same boat." Reimagining the world, challenging the dominant visual regime, and expanding our imagination are difficult tasks. If we do not accomplish them, then all we are left with is a dystopic future—one that may already have begun.

Translated from the German by Jacqueline Todd

+   Daniel Neugebauer is head of the Department of Communications and Cultural Education at Haus der Kulturen der Welt. Educated as a literary scholar, he is interested in the interfaces of communication and educational work. Having trained at the Kunsthalle Bielefeld, from 2012 to 2018 he headed the division of marketing, mediation, and fundraising at the Van Abbemuseum in the Netherlands. In 2016/17 he coordinated marketing for documenta 14 in Kassel and Athens. In recent years, inclusion and queering have been the focus of his institutional practice.

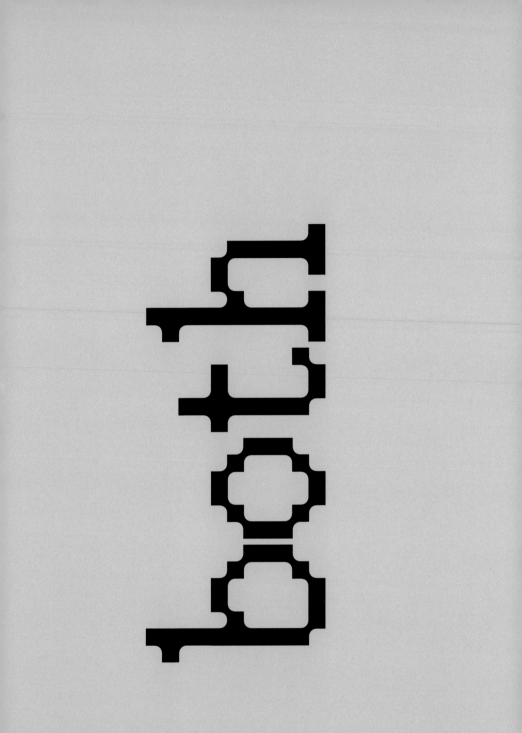

about times

+   Olympia Bukkakis is a drag and dance artist. In 2009, she started to perform in Melbourne, Australia. Since moving to Berlin in 2012 she has organized various queer performance nights in the city, including *Get Fucked, Apocalypse Tonight*, and *Queens Against Borders*. In 2018, she completed the Solo/Dance/Authorship (SODA) Master's degree at HZT Berlin with her piece *Tales From a State of Shemergency*. Her piece *Gender Euphoria* celebrated its premiere at the Sophiensæle within the *Tanztage Berlin* 2019. Most recently she showed: *Work on Progress* (HAU festival, Hebbel am Ufer theater, Berlin), *Under Pressures* (Gessnerallee theater, Zurich), *Boys Night Out* (Abbotsford Convent, Melbourne), and *A Touch of the Other* (Sophiensæle, Berlin).

+   María do Mar Castro Varela is Professor of Pedagogy and Social Work at the Alice Salomon Hochschule Berlin (ASH Berlin). She holds a double degree in psychology and pedagogy, and a PhD in political science. Besides critical migration research and forced migration studies, her key professional and research interests are postcolonial theory, critical education, and issues related to gender and queer studies. Her publications include *Postkoloniale Theorie. Eine kritische Einführung* (2005), and *Migrationspädagogik* (2010).

+   Rain Demetri creates works inspired by "rubber hose" animation, animals, and the surreal. She favors using ballpoint pens, acrylic, gouache, clay, and software applications to make humorous and ghoulish monsters. Much of her work is also derived from traditional art, dark art concepts, and caricature techniques. She explores whimsical and grotesque themes influenced by behaviors in nature and the imagination. Through her absurd and imaginary beasts, Rain seeks to create works that disrupt the definition of beauty and celebrate lowbrow art.

+   Sabine Mohamed is a PhD candidate in anthropology at Heidelberg University and at the Max Planck Institute for the Study of Religious and Ethnic Diversity in Göttingen. Her dissertation explores processes of urbanization, Black empire,

temporality, and the inscription of ethnic difference in urban
Ethiopia. Mohamed's research interests include themes of
representation, the circulation of ideas, race/Blackness, and
the body. She is a member of Mädchenmannschaft, a German-
language, feminist blog collective, and also plays an active
role in the bildungsLab*.

+   Bonaventure Soh Bejeng Ndikung is an independent
curator, author, and biotechnologist. He is the founder and
artistic director of SAVVY Contemporary Berlin. He was curator-
at-large at documenta 14 in Athens and Kassel, artistic director
of the 12th Rencontres de Bamako 2019, guest curator at the
Dak'Art Biennale in Senegal 2018, curated the Finnish Pavilion
at the 58th Venice Biennale 2019 together with the Miracle
Workers Collective, and is artistic director of Sonsbeek 2020–
2024. He has been a visiting professor for curatorial studies
and sound art at the Städelschule in Frankfurt and is also the
recipient of the first OCAD University International Curators
Residency (ICR) fellowship in Toronto 2020. He is currently a
professor in the MA program in spatial strategies at the Kunst-
hochschule Weißensee in Berlin.

+   Olave Nduwanje is a jurist and queer, anti-racist, feminist
activist. Olave fled from Burundi to the Netherlands in the early
1990s. Olave identifies as a Black, non-binary trans femme
and addict in recovery. She is an author, organizer, performer
and speaker and was a 2017 parliamentary candidate in the
Netherlands for Bij1, the first openly intersectional feminist party
in Europe founded by a Black woman, Sylvana Simons. Her
interview series *Olave Talks* aims for highlighting knowledge
production, strategies and tools developed by fellow and
intersectional queer feminists.

+   Jules Sturm is a senior researcher in Art Education at the
Zürcher Hochschule der Künste (ZHdK, Zurich University of
the Arts) and teaches critical studies at the Sandberg Instituut,
Amsterdam. Jules has taught literary theory and cultural
analysis at the University of Amsterdam. Originally trained
in philosophy and women's studies, Jules specialized in critical

theories of the body in Art and Aesthetics, Queer Studies, Post-human Theories, and Critical Disability Studies. Jules' interests engage with embodied theories and alternative knowledge production in contemporary culture and education, aiming towards committed forms of learning from, within, and beyond diversity.

+ Julius Thissen is an artist and artistic researcher working with a wide range of media: performance, photography, film, sculpture, and scent. The works investigate notions of community and representation, masculinity, sports, and competition. With the work, Thissen aims to create narratives that investigate the fine line between performing and failing. These relations are strongly linked to contemporary performance-driven culture and the influence of social expectations on our behavior. The work also relates to personal experiences as a genderqueer, transmasculine individual, as, emerging from these experiences, Julius strongly challenges the constraining narratives imposed on transgender and queer people. Thissen is based in Arnhem in the Netherlands.

Colophon

Das Neue Alphabet (The New Alphabet) is a publication series by HKW (Haus der Kulturen der Welt).

The series is part of the HKW project *Das Neue Alphabet* (2019–2022), supported by the Federal Government Commissioner for Culture and the Media due to a ruling of the German Bundestag.

Series Editors: Detlef Diederichsen, Anselm Franke, Katrin Klingan, Daniel Neugebauer, Bernd Scherer
Project Management: Philipp Albers
Managing Editor: Martin Hager
Copy-Editing: Mandi Gomez, Hannah Sarid de Mowbray
Design Concept: Olaf Nicolai with Malin Gewinner and Hannes Drißner

Vol. 3: *Counter_Readings of the Body*
Editor: Daniel Neugebauer
Coordination: Laida Hadel
Contributors: Olympia Bukkakis, María do Mar Castro Varela, Rain Demetri, Sabine Mohamed, Bonaventure Soh Bejeng Ndikung, Olave Nduwanje, Jules Sturm, Julius Thissen
Translations: Kevin Kennedy, Jacqueline Todd
Graphic Design: Malin Gewinner, Hannes Drißner, Markus Dreßen
Type-Setting: Hannah Witte
Fonts: FK Raster (Florian Karsten), Suisse BP Int'l (Ian Party), Lyon Text (Kai Bernau)
Image Editing: Scancolor Reprostudio GmbH, Leipzig
Printing and Binding: Gutenberg Beuys Feindruckerei GmbH, Langenhagen

Published by:
Spector Books
Harkortstr. 10
01407 Leipzig
www.spectorbooks.com

Distribution:
Germany, Austria: GVA Gemeinsame Verlagsauslieferung
        Göttingen GmbH & Co. KG, www.gva-verlage.de
Switzerland: AVA Verlagsauslieferung AG, www.ava.ch
France, Belgium: Interart Paris, www.interart.fr
UK: Central Books Ltd, www.centralbooks.com
USA, Canada, Central and South America, Africa:
        ARTBOOK | D.A.P. www.artbook.com
Japan: twelvebooks, www.twelve-books.com
South Korea: The Book Society, www.thebooksociety.org
Australia, New Zealand: Perimeter Distribution,
        www.perimeterdistribution.com

Haus der Kulturen der Welt
John-Foster-Dulles-Allee 10
D-10557 Berlin
www.hkw.de

Haus der Kulturen der Welt is a business division of Kultur-
veranstaltungen des Bundes in Berlin GmbH (KBB).

Director: Bernd Scherer
Managing Director: Charlotte Sieben
Chairwoman of the Supervisory Board: Federal Government
        Commissioner for Culture and the Media
        Prof. Monika Grütters MdB

Haus der Kulturen der Welt is supported by

Minister of State
for Culture and the Media

Federal Foreign Office

First Edition
Printed in Germany
ISBN: 978-3-95905-459-1

Recently published:
Vol. 1: *The New Alphabet*
Vol. 2: *Listen to Lists*
Vol. 3: *Counter_Readings of the Body*

Forthcoming:
Vol. 4: *Echo* (February 2021)
Vol. 5: *Skin and Code* (March 2021)
Vol. 6: *Carrier Bag Fiction* (April 2021)

Vol. 4:   *Echo*
Editors: Nick Houde, Katrin Klingan, Johanna Schindler
Contrib.:   Lisa Baraitser, Louis Chude-Sokei, Maya Indira
             Ganesh, Wesley Goatley, Xavier Le Roy,
             Luciana Parisi, Sascha Pohflepp, Sophia Roosth,
             Gary Thomlinson
ISBN: 978-3-95905-457-7
             February 2021

"If sound is birth and silence death, the echo trailing into infinity can only be the experience of life, the source of narrative and a pattern for history." Drawing on Louis Chude-Sokei's metaphorical, political, and technopoetic investigations, this volume experiments with how the echo of past ideas of life and form has brought forth the technologies and lifestyles that our contemporary world is based on. The essays, conversations, and artist contributions delineate a variegated array of technologies, creating an image of their past and their future potentials.

Vol. 5:   *Skin and Code*
Editor: Daniel Neugebauer
Contrib.:   Alyk Blue, Luce deLire, i-Päd, Rhea Ramjohn,
             Julia Velkova & Anne Kaun
ISBN: 978-3-95905-461-4
             March 2021

Just as physical violence leaves its marks on the skin, conceptual violence is written into interfaces via algorithms—in the form of biases turned into pixels, as discrimination implanted in memes in secret chat groups. The coding and decoding of body surfaces and interfaces is contingent on a whole host of norms. Yet these are not fixed: rather, they combine to create a matrix of tastes, cultural influences, technical conditions, and physical possibilities. The essays in this volume produce an interdisciplinary noise between surface structures and a selection of cavities: surfaces, skins, and interfaces are injured, gauged, altered, or remedied.

Vol. 6:   *Carrier Bag Fiction*
Editors: Sarah Shin, Mathias Zeiske
Contrib.:   Federico Campagna, Dorothee Elmiger,
            Ursula K. Le Guin, Enis Maci a. o.
ISBN: 978-3-95905-463-8
            April 2021

What if humanity's primary inventions were not the Hero's spear but rather a basket of wild oats, a medicine bundle, a story. Ursula K. Le Guin's 1986 essay *The Carrier Bag Theory of Fiction* presents a feminist story of technology that centres on the collective sustenance of life, and reimagines the carrier bag as a tool for telling strangely realistic fictions. New writings and images respond to Le Guin's narrative practice of world-making through gathering and holding.